Rhythms Of My Young Heart

J. E. Lindsay

First published in Northern Ireland in 2017
by Excalibur Press

Copyright © 2017 J. E. Lindsay

All rights reserved.
No part of this publication may be reproduced, stored in a retrieval system, or transmitted, in any form or by any means (electronic, mechanical, photocopying, recording or otherwise) without the prior permission of the publisher and copyright holder, nor be otherwise circulated in any form of binding or cover other than that in which it is published.

ISBN: 978-1-910728-32-1

Formatting & layout by
Excalibur Press

Excalibur Press
Belfast, Northern Ireland

team@excaliburpress.co.uk
07982628911 | @ExcaliburPress
www.excaliburpress.co.uk

For Rory..... I finally found you x

CONTENTS

	Foreword	5
1	Growing Up	6
2	Dangerous	7
3	What Have You Done For Me	8
4	Religion	9
5	Quench My Thirst	10
6	You	11
7	Getting Rid Of You	12
8	My Heart Was	13
9	My Future Husband	14
10	Tonight	15
11	First Love	16
12	It's Not Your Fault	17
13	Angel	18
14	Angel - Pt 2	19
15	Nothing Without You	20
16	My Cloud	21
17	Prayer For A Lost Love	22
18	No One Expects An Angel To Die	23
19	Lost Love	24
20	Impossible	25
	About The Author	26

Foreword

I feel that writing has always been a part of my anatomy. For as long as I can remember, I've been writing poetry, short stories and songs for my own entertainment. I find poetry - both reading and writing it - to be very therapeutic. Through poetry, we can take our innermost feelings, thoughts and desires, and turn them into something beautiful – something that other people can relate to.

The poems in this book were written throughout my teenage years, when I was dealing with first love, first heartache and everything in between. Emotions can run high with teenagers, and I felt that poetry was a healthy, creative and rewarding outlet for all the emotions I was feeling at that time.

I have also included a poem not written as a teenager – a dedication to Michael Jackson that I wrote after his death. Michael Jackson's music has been a huge inspiration to me throughout my whole life. He inspired me to connect to my own creativity and without him, there is a large possibility that none of these poems would exist.

J. E. Lindsay

GROWING UP

Running faster towards my fate.

Racing against the speed of heart rate.

Trying to keep at a steady pace

While hurtling into space.

Seeing my childhood pass me by.

Flying like a bird towards the sky.

My life is soaring away

Here and gone, in what seems a day.

What once to me, was oh so dear

Is dripping away in a lonely tear.

I try so hard to stop my cries

But it's hard to kiss my youth goodbye.

Dangerous

I don't want to move when I'm in his hands

There's nothing I can do to get away.

I can't leave 'cos I cancelled all my plans

And I told everyone that I'm away.

He is so bad but he feels so good

I'll be everything he needs.

I never know what he's thinking

Or what he's going to do.

His very blink is a sign of danger

And I give in and feel like a fool.

He's my secret, but I scream him out loud.

I'll be everything he wants.

WHAT HAVE YOU DONE FOR ME

What have you done for me lately?
Except numb the pain
Of love lost
And hurt gained.

What have you done for me lately?
Except dry the tears
That drowned my happiness
And aroused my fears.

What have you done for me lately?
Except heal the scars.
Left behind
By long lonely hours.

What have you done for me lately?
Except dress the wounds
Caused by singing
An agonising tune.

What have you done for me lately?
Everything.

Religion

Silence the church bells

Hush the church choir

Mute the priest

For he is a liar.

Quench My Thirst

I'm drowning in a deep ocean

Of your brown eyes.

I'm swimming in a vast pool

Of your love.

I'm floating in a quiet stream

Of emotions.

I'm sinking in a peaceful lake

Of happiness and joy.

I'm bathing in a wide river

Of lust for you.

I'm showering in a nourishing waterfall

Of your perfect smile.

You quench my thirst for you.

You

As the tears fall down my cheeks
We kiss for the last time
And say goodbye.
My first love, my true love, my only love.
You know I will love you
Until my time slips away.
As your lips part
To say goodbye one final time
I close my finger over your tender mouth
And wish you well.
Knowing I will never see you again,
I die on the inside.
In my mind, I curl up in a corner
And slowly fade away to nothing,
Because without you I am nothing.
Without you, what am I?
Tell me.
Why do I exist in this world,
When I am only a feeble nothing?
I'm on the verge of dying
Because you are my oxygen
And now you're gone.
You are my everything
And now I'm alone.

Getting Rid Of You

I've been so many different places.

Seen so many different faces.

But when I met you, my life stood still from then.

Because of you, why must my life end?

You came into my life, boasting the best

But you can play that trick on someone else.

Because I'm not here to messed around

And have my heart placed in the lost and found.

If you think I'm staying to hear you moan

Think again, or you'll be alone!

I'm not a puppet for you to hold on a string.

I am my own person, I do my own thing!

You cannot tell me what I can and cannot do.

Because before it's too late, I'm getting rid of you!

MY HEART WAS

My heart was once a rock

Until you smashed it to tiny stones.

My heart was once a house.

Until you shattered it to a pile of bricks.

My heart was once a forest

Until you burned it to just a tree.

My heart was once a heart

Until you broke it on me.

My Future Husband

I often sit and wonder
Who he will be.
And when I think about him
Does he think about me?
I lie in bed at night
Thinking about my future life
And I think about the man
Who will make me his wife.
Will we be meeting soon?
Or have we already met?
Will we meet tomorrow?
Have I to meet him yet?
Will we get along at first?
Or will I hate him so?
Not knowing that I'll learn to love him,
Will I treat him like a foe?
I long to know this man
And know who he will be.
And when I think about him,
Does he think about me?

Tonight

Tonight I'll give my heart away
But before I do
Promise you'll take care of it
If I give it away to you.

Tonight I'll hold you in my arms
But before I do
Promise me you'll hold me too
If I hold you.

Tonight I'll want to kiss you
But before I do
Promise me you'll kiss me back
If I kiss you.

Tonight I'll share a secret
But before I do
Promise me you'll listen
If I tell my secret to you.

Tonight will be so special
But before it is
Promise me you'll feel it too
If I make it special
Just for you.

First Love

I want to keep this simple
But there's so much I could say.
Missing you gets harder
And harder every day

The closer we get
The further I hide.
I'm afraid to commit
And I don't know why.

I want to get close to you
I want us to be,
But I don't understand why
The thought of you makes me weak.

I try to be calm for you
As calm as I can be
But I just can't help
Wanting you here with me.

I want you to know
That this is hard for me to say.
I've never had to express this.
I've never felt this way.

I'm falling more
In love with you each day
I don't want this to ever change
I love my life this way.

It's Not Your Fault

It's not your fault
That I feel in love
But it is your fault
That I'm hurt.
You made me feel
So beautiful inside.
But now I feel the worst.
It's not your fault
That I get butterflies
Each time I hear your name
But it is your fault
That I'm lonely,
Because you think love is a game.
It's not your fault
That I want you here
But it is your fault
That you're gone.
I tried so hard to hold you
But it seems that you've moved on.
It's not your fault
That I love you
But it is your fault
That you'll never know.
You never gave us a chance together.
And now my love can't grow.

Angel

There was an angel in Heaven

And God sent him to me,

Knowing that my arms

Are where he should be.

He held me and kissed me

And he loved me so much

And now nothing can compare

To my angels sweet touch.

Angel - Pt 2

I'm trying to find words

That don't exist

To describe these feelings

That my heart can't resist.

But I realise that poetry

Is pointless with you

Because no matter what words I use

They will never be true.

I love you more than I could ever say

And my love for you grows

With each passing day.

Nothing Without You

The sun was shining before
But now the sky wreaks of rain.
My tears are disguised as droplets
And my eyes are filled with pain.

The solitude inside of me
Pours out from within my soul
And although I try to hide it inside
Without you here – I don't feel whole.

My arms reach out
To touch your skin
But they hang, empty, in the air.
The void that has now surrendered my soul
It seems, will always be there.

My Cloud

Don't make me come down
From my cloud.
Let me stay here
Out of reality's reach.
Let me sail in emancipation
Over the globe
Amidst these heavenly surroundings.
Let me dream of what it's like
To not be locked up
In this prison of affection
That exists
Only in my imagination.
Let me float above the earth
For just a minute more.
I'm desperately hanging on
To this one last thread.
Please help me never forget
What it feels like
To be in love.

Prayer For A Lost Love

Dear God
I'm in love with a man
Who doesn't love me back.
Can you understand my pain?
Can you help me with that?
I'm sure with your powers
You can change his mind.
You can make him want me.
You can make him be mine.
You gave him to me
He was mine for two years
But you took him away again
And left me in tears.
Can you please bring him back to me?
This man I love so much
I want to be his lover again
And I'm longing for his touch.
Woman to woman
Will you please do all you can?
To bring my lover back to me
And reunite me with my man.
Amen.

No One Expects An Angel To Die

No one expects an angel to die
To just grow wings and fly.
No one expects it, but now everyone knows
How hard it is, when an angel goes.
Everyone loves you, but no one knew
Just how much, until you flew.
Like the sun in the sky, you made the world shine bright.
Now we gaze upon your star, as you light up the night.
Masses flocked to hear your song.
And in our hearts, you will live on.
I close my eyes to see your face
But that's all I could ever do in the first place.
Gone in body, but never in soul
You'll stay in our hearts, because no one else can fill the hole.
The earth was awash with your beauty and glow
Now Heaven is host to your spirit and soul.
Fly by our sides, you're the reason we're together.
In your fans hearts you are alive, and you will be forever.

R.I.P Michael Joseph Jackson

Lost Love

I promised you forever
And I meant every word
You had the key to my heart
Then you shattered my world.

My life without you
Feels empty and cold
I want you with me forever
I want our future to unfold.

You walked out on our future
And left my world torn apart
You told me I was the one
And then you broke my heart.

I've never felt like this before
I've never felt so broken.
I want to know your thoughts and feelings
I want to hear those words that are unspoken.

I loved you more than life
I needed you more than air
You made me believe that I had everything
Then you proved you didn't care.

What if we could talk it over?
Could you tell me where we went wrong?
I need to know what led to this
Only then can I truly move on.

Impossible

It's easy to forget
What our love meant.
It's easy to believe
That you needed to leave.
It's easy to say
That you prefer it this way,
But it's impossible to find
Another like me!

It's easy to pretend
That you're glad it's the end.
It's easy to feel
That you're happiness is real.
It's easy to enjoy
Being a single boy,
But it's impossible to find
Another like me!

About The Author

J.E. Lindsay is a married mum of two with a passion for creative writing going back as long as she can remember. Throughout her school years, she was constantly praised for her short stories and imaginative anecdotes, and consequently started writing short stories as a hobby.

As a teenager, she began writing poetry, and has had two poems published in an Anthology of Poetry which was published in America.

This is her first published book, and will be closely followed by a crime thriller novel 'Dr Kingston'.

www.ingramcontent.com/pod-product-compliance
Lightning Source LLC
Chambersburg PA
CBHW061317040426
42444CB00010B/2679